Original title:
The Shores of Paradise

Copyright © 2025 Creative Arts Management OÜ
All rights reserved.

Author: Gabriel Kingsley
ISBN HARDBACK: 978-1-80581-577-8
ISBN PAPERBACK: 978-1-80581-104-6
ISBN EBOOK: 978-1-80581-577-8

The Dance of Elysian Tides

Waves tango with the sun's warm glow,
Seagulls join in, putting on a show.
Crabs break dance, without a care,
Shells clap their hands, what a sight rare!

Sandcastles tiptoe, proud and tall,
While beach balls bounce, having a ball.
Flip-flops parade, marching on by,
With sunscreen as drums, they're aiming high.

Radiant Echoes of the Salted Breeze

Breezes weave tales from the ocean deep,
Where mermaids giggle and dolphins leap.
Surfboards are surfers' trusty steeds,
Riding the wave of laughter's needs.

Kites soar high like dreams untamed,
While beach umbrellas play hide-and-seek, unclaimed.
Fried food carts sing their greasy tune,
Inviting all for a feast 'neath the moon.

Journey to the Enchanted Coast

Buckets and shovels in each tiny hand,
Building dreams in this sandy land.
A seagull swoops, stealing a fry,
Leaving kids to gasp and sigh!

Picnics spread out; ants join the fun,
Chasing crumbs under a blazing sun.
Icy treats drip, oh what a mess,
Giggles burst forth—sweet summertime stress!

A Symphony of Sunlit Sands

Footprints swirl like a dance parade,
Sandcastle walls slowly degrade.
As waves retreat, they whisper soft,
While children scream, 'Watch me lift off!'

Tanning lotion's a slippery foe,
As laughter erupts, it's a slippery show.
Sun-hats tumble, tossed with glee,
In this symphony, we are wild and free!

Whispers of Celestial Waters

In the land where mermaids roam,
They always ask for your phone.
With selfies snapped, they take a dive,
While seagulls laugh and jive.

Bubbles rise like gossip tales,
Fish join in with silly wails.
Even crabs have their own gig,
As they dance a tiny jig.

Lost in the Embrace of Eternal Waves

A beach ball flew, it took a ride,
While I sat dumbfounded inside.
My sunscreen failed to guard my nose,
Now it's red, like a garden rose.

The sand got stuck between my toes,
I tried to dance, but lost my pose.
Seagulls swooped with mischief spread,
Stealing fries right from my head.

Beyond the Glistening Horizon

A treasure map leads to the sea,
With X marking snacks, just for me.
But the only gold I found tonight,
Was a can of soda, cold and bright.

The waves play tricks like they're my pals,
Slapstick moments, splashy brawls.
I navigate through salty air,
While crabs applaud my great despair.

Echoes of Heaven's Edge

In flip-flops, I thought I'd fly,
But all I did was nearly cry.
With a splash and a dive, oh what a sight,
I mistook my towel for a kite!

Laughter echoed from the sand,
As I wrestled with ice cream, oh so grand.
Sprinkles everywhere, what a mess!
But somehow it feels like pure success.

Secrets of the Moonlit Shore

Nights so bright, the crabs do dance,
In moonlit glow, they take their chance.
A starfish in a tiny hat,
Claims he's the king, now how 'bout that?

Waves that giggle, tickle toes,
Shells with secrets only they know.
An octopus with funny shoes,
Sells ice cream on the ocean blues.

Caresses of Salt and Sun

The sun tells jokes to the salty sea,
While gulls laugh loud, oh let it be!
A sardine secretly plays the lute,
Rehearsing tunes for a fishy pursuit.

Dolphins dive with a splashy cheer,
Waving at swimmers with no fear.
A crab with shades just chills in style,
While sandcastles fear the tide's grim smile.

The Legend of the Mystic Bay

In a bay where mermaids lose their combs,
Fishermen search for abandoned homes.
A sea turtle busts a move, so slick,
Breaking the waves with a funny trick.

Tales of pirates who can't find gold,
Instead, they chase their hats, so bold.
The winds howl jokes, the waves all clap,
As sharks don bow ties for a fancy nap.

Requiem for the Distant Isle

A distant isle with bananas bold,
Its mysteries wrapped in stories old.
Parrots debate if the sun's too bright,
While iguanas take a midday flight.

Coconuts drop like falling stars,
As beach balls float to Jupiter's bars.
A crab's retirement is quite the tale,
He runs a cafe with fish on sale.

The Language of the Seafoam

In bubbly tongues, the sea did speak,
A fish with dreams, so bold, so sleek.
It shared a tale of salty squabbles,
Where crabs held grudges, and seashells wobbled.

The gulls would cackle, a loud parade,
As waves performed their grand charade.
"Who knew," they said, "seaweed could dance?
Let's join the fun, let's take a chance!"

Hushed Murmurs of the Island Breeze

A whisper floats on the island air,
A coconut's gossip, oh so rare.
"Did you see that wave? It wore a hat!
And the sandcastles? They were all that!"

Palm leaves giggle, swaying slow,
Tickling each other, putting on a show.
The breeze hums tunes of playful schemes,
While turtles plot their dream-like dreams.

Cradles of Moonlight

The moonlit waves rocked boats to sleep,
Stars winked at fish that would laugh and leap.
A seagull's choir, off-key yet spry,
Made nightingale blush as it flew by.

With laughter in hearts and light on their fins,
Octopuses twirled, showing off their spins.
As constellations danced in the warm, salty glow,
The ocean's humor was quite the show!

Legends Carved in Driftwood

A driftwood log told tales of old,
Of pirates who sneezed at treasures of gold.
"Beware," it chuckled, "of maps that mislead,
Or cats who pretend, yes, they're poets indeed!"

With bark bits of wisdom, it spoke with flair,
Of beachcombers searching for socks, what a scare!
The legend grew wild, like a myth in the night,
Driftwood's jokes, a true comedic delight!

Serene Horizon's Call

On a breeze that smells like fries,
Seagulls dive with goofy cries.
Surfboards wobble, but we grin,
As sand gets stuck under our skin.

Ice cream drips, oh what a mess,
Life's too short, let's just confess.
A turtle laughs as he rolls by,
In this place where time can fly.

Odes to Lost Horizons

Where flip-flops wander, lost in sand,
A crab gives directions—oh so grand!
We follow the waves, then trip and fall,
Not quite elegant, but we have a ball.

The sun aims for a golden tan,
While seaweed wraps around our plan.
With giggles loud and visions hazy,
This silly trip just makes us crazy.

Lullabies of the Emerald Sea

The ocean hums a silly tune,
While dolphins dance beneath the moon.
We chat with fish, they nod and sway,
As crabs throw sand our way to play.

Beach umbrellas like mushrooms bloom,
Our laughter fills the salty room.
A mermaid winks, with scales so bright,
As waves crash down in sheer delight.

Journeying to the Tranquil Edge

A treasure map drawn in ketchup stains,
Leads us to shores without constraints.
Where flip-flops fly and drinks are poured,
Adventure waits; we can't be ignored.

Shady palms gossip in the breeze,
While crabs do the cha-cha with ease.
With sunburned noses and joyful hearts,
This wacky journey, oh how it starts!

The Call of Horizon's Embrace

The sun does a dance, wearing shades so bright,
While seagulls argue who's got the best flight.
Sandy toes wiggle, a crab plots his heist,
Laughing at humans who think they're the nicest.

A dolphin does flips, with a wink at my snack,
As I try to relax, the waves pull me back.
Flip-flops and sunburn, oh what a delight,
Life's little mischief keeps me up every night.

A Haven of Endless Wonders

In this beachy realm, I lost my last shoe,
A fish stole my sandwich, it's true, oh it's true!
Jellyfish bobbing like they own the whole bay,
While I trip over towels, my beach day ballet.

Kites sailing high, like they're in a race,
Kids building castles, with mud on their face.
Each wave tells a joke, as they crash on the sand,
The ocean's alive with a slapstick band.

Ripples of Timeless Bliss

The tide comes in, like a sneaky old thief,
Stealing my snack while I'm pondering grief.
Mermaids giggle, as they braid their long hair,
Plotting to give me a splash and a scare!

With seagulls gossiping, what a raucous fit,
"Did you see that guy? He totally fell in it!"
No one's quite graceful, we all wobble a bit,
Yet laughter erupts, and we all laugh and sit.

Whims of the Ocean's Heart

The ocean waves whistle, a quirky old tune,
While I chase a beach ball, oh how it's a boon!
Bikini tops flying, a fashion faux pas,
As everyone stares, I just giggle and caw.

Starfish winking, they've seen it all before,
Shells whisper secrets, surf's laughter galore.
With every splash, there's a tale to unfold,
Of summer silliness, worth more than gold.

Harbors of Tranquility

In a beach chair I sit back,
With a drink that's a colorful snack,
The sun has a grin so right,
Even seagulls are taking flight.

A crab steals my sandwich in glee,
As I shout, "Hey, you can't dine on me!"
But he dances away on the sand,
With my lunch firmly held in his hand.

Embraced by the Sea's Caress

Waves come in like a playful pup,
Each splash a hug, then a hiccup,
I try to dance with the tide,
But my balance has taken a slide.

A fish jumps up like a cheerleader,
While I find my shorts could be neater,
Laughter echoes across the shore,
As I slip, my body at war.

The Palette of the Tide

Colors swirl in the evening light,
As folks juggle their fries with delight,
A seagull swoops down in a dive,
And steals a hot dog; oh, what a drive!

Children giggle, their buckets in hand,
While building a castle made of wet sand,
A wave crashes down with a roar,
And the castle is gone—oh, there's the score!

Secrets Written in Sands of Time

Footprints trace a silly dance,
As I twist and shout, trying to prance,
But I trip on a shell, oh dear me,
And now I'm a part of the sea!

Shells whisper tales from long ago,
Of mermaids that taught them how to flow,
But they giggle at my awkward stance,
And join the sea in a merry dance.

Tales from the Boundless Lagoon

In a lagoon where fish wear hats,
The seagulls critique like old chatty rats.
Crabs dance the tango on the sandy floor,
While octopuses juggle—who could ask for more?

A sunburnt frog plays a banjo tune,
As turtles tumble under a fat, grinning moon.
The jellyfish glow like disco balls bright,
Encouraging all to dance through the night.

Treasures of the Infinite Shore

A squirrel found gold on the endless sand,
But it turned out to be just a broken band.
Seashells lined up for a chorus routine,
While starfish offered a fine cappuccino machine.

The waves played chess with the lazy old rocks,
As seahorses debated in their fancy frocks.
A clam tried to sing but was all out of tune,
Leaving crabs to applaud and howl at the moon.

Serenity Where the Sea Meets the Sky

Where bubbles burst into giggling fits,
And dolphins throw parties with shimmying skits.
Pelicans juggling shrimp in a show,
While shrimp shout, "Hey! We're the stars of the flow!"

A wise old walrus dispensed sage advice,
Like, "Never trust fish that are too cold as ice."
The parrot squawked jokes that made everyone cheer,
As the tide tried to steal his bright-colored beer.

Tranquil Embers of Distant Shores

On distant shores where the sunsets glow,
Seagulls enact plays that steal the show.
A whale's got a tattoo, it's quite a delight,
Of a shipwrecked pogo stick—oh what a sight!

The sands hold secrets of past sandy fights,
Where crabs wear headbands for competitive nights.
Beach umbrellas flutter like wild calls for aid,
While the tide keeps mumbling—"I'm totally paid!"

Celestial Currents and Quiet Dreams

Under a sky of jellybeans,
The waves tap dance, oh what a scene!
A fish in a tux with a top hat too,
Winks at the sun with a cheeky 'Boo!'

Seagulls gossip in comedic flight,
Dropping their snacks, what a funny sight!
As crabs wear shades, lounging in sand,
They sizzle like bacon, oh isn't this grand?

The breeze tells jokes with a flirty spin,
Catching our laughter as if it could win.
While shells hold secrets, whispers of glee,
Entrapping the giggles of you and me.

When twilight sparkles with winkled stars,
The octopus DJ spins tunes from afar.
Dancing till dawn, we stumble and sway,
In this fin-tastic dreamland, let's giggle and play!

Sanctuary of the Forgotten Waves

In a cove where the sand tickles toes,
A hermit crab juggles its home, as it goes.
With a wink and a wave, it shows off its shell,
It's a rolling hotel, can you just tell?

Seashells gossip with stories untold,
Of clams with wild parties, so silly and bold.
They whisper of sailors who danced on the shore,
To a tune only starfish can properly score.

The seaweed wiggles, a comical dance,
As fish in tuxedos, strike up a romance.
They giggle at waves that try to impress,
With splashes of foam, it's a quirky success!

As tides blend horizons in laughter and light,
The sunsets chuckle, a glorious sight.
In this sanctuary of whimsy and play,
Forgotten waves echo the joy of our day!

Reflections on the Alabaster Coast

On the bright rocks where crabs have a blast,
A pelican dives, wins the day—such a cast!
With feathers all ruffled and beak in a twist,
It makes the biggest splash, oh what a list!

Seashells line up to form a parade,
As barnacles boast of the friends that they've made.
The tide plays piano, each wave a new note,
Inviting all creatures to join in the boat.

Clouds in formations compete for the crown,
While dolphins breakdance, wearing smiles, oh wow!
They flip and they plop, with a giggly cheer,
As everyone watches, just wishing to steer.

Reflections of laughter ripple on by,
In the glow of the dusk, we'll savor the sky.
This coast is a canvas of joy without end,
Where the humor of nature is always a friend!

The Magic of Distant Horizons

At the edge of the world where the sun likes to play,
The horizon winks at the end of the day.
Fish wear their shades, strutting with glee,
While crabs roll their carts of fresh jubilee!

A pelican shows off its trendy new dive,
Teaching the starfish how to feel alive.
With a splash and a laugh, the ocean complies,
As foam tickles toes, oh how time flies!

Where clouds float like pillows, the seagulls unite,
Throwing a party in the fading sunlight.
With each goofy squawk, they make quite the scene,
Dancing on waves, they keep it serene.

So here on this shore, where humor's the key,
We learn from the sea to be joyful and free.
With each new horizon that giggles and sways,
We find the true magic in playful displays!

A Symphony of Tides

The seaweed dances in delight,
While crabs perform their crabby fight.
Seagulls squawk a silly song,
With clam shells clapping all day long.

Beach balls bounce in wild parade,
Sandy toes make quite the trade.
Umbrellas turn like tipsy hats,
As dolphins shine and throw cheeky jabs.

In the sun, a lizard struts,
While kids in flip-flops trip in ruts.
The waves applaud with foamy cheer,
And jellyfish wink, oh-so-clear.

So grab your floaties, skip on down,
Join the party, wear a crown.
In this playful tide, we glide,
As giggles ride the surging tide.

The Secret Cove's Embrace

In a cove where seashells sneak,
A crab calls out with a cheeky squeak.
Flip-flops fly like birds in flight,
While sunscreened faces laugh with delight.

Fishes gossip, sharing tales,
Beneath the surface, giggles sail.
An octopus plays hide and seek,
Pretending to be a lazy creek.

A picnic spread on a blanket bright,
Sandwiches wiggle, a silly sight.
Cupcakes frolic on plastic plates,
Dancing round just like the mates.

With lemonade laughter in the air,
The sun melts worries, like a fair.
In our secret little cove,
Silliness and joy we'll always stow.

Where Dreams Kiss the Sand

A castle made of dreams and foam,
Where mermaids come to call it home.
Starfish whisper to the shells,
As laughter rings like tinkling bells.

A kite takes flight, a colorful spree,
While children leap with glee by the sea.
In the backdrop, clowns on boards,
Surfing waves, ruling the fjords.

Bucket lists fly, with a squee,
Shovels digging for treasure glee.
A squirrel in sunglasses strikes a pose,
While sunbathers get sunburned noses.

The horizon blushes, painted bright,
As the day dances into the night.
Where dreams do meet and laughter lands,
In this place where joy never strands.

Echoes of a Sunlit Realm

Echoes bounce from wave to shore,
As seagulls giggle, wanting more.
Flip-flops clatter, a merry tune,
While we chase crabs beneath the moon.

The sand tickles our toes and lips,
As ice cream melts, a drippy trip.
Towels balloon like parachutes,
While kids aspire to win the loot.

A sandcastle tournament takes its lead,
With moats and flags, oh what a deed!
Twisted towels form silly hats,
And laughter echoes, bouncing back.

Driftwood waits, a throne for kings,
As magic, laughter, and summer sings.
In this sunlit realm, joy prevails,
As life's funny moments fill our sails.

Candlelit Waves and Skylit Dreams

The moon's a disco ball, so bright,
Crabs dance under starlit light.
Seagulls gossip, tales so tall,
While I trip over my beach ball.

Cocktails spill, oh what a scene,
Sunburned noses, red and green.
My beach chair's lost to ghostly tides,
While laughter surfs, our worries slide.

Flip-flops flap with each bold stride,
We chase the waves, our hearts a-glide.
Sandcastles lean like tipsy friends,
As giggles rise, the fun never ends.

Mermaids tease with salty grins,
Tequila shots in giant fins.
With every wave, our spirits rise,
On this shore, we find our prize.

The Scent of Ocean Whispers

Inhale the breeze, it smells like fries,
While seagulls cackle, oh how they cry.
The salty air brings lots of cheer,
And fishy tales from yesteryear.

The tide rolls in, flirtatious myths,
Like finding treasure, or that lost fifth.
We dive for shells, just one more try,
But come up with seaweed, oh my, oh my!

Beach balls bounce and sunscreen's thick,
As kids build towers on the quick.
The golden sand, our squishy throne,
Where laughter echoes, joy is sown.

Gossiping surfers ride the swells,
Spitting water as each one yells.
With every wave, hilarity flows,
On this beach, anything goes!

The Allure of Lost Beaches

A map of sand, we lost our way,
With crabs as guides, we'll surely play.
A shell treasure hunt, what a find,
Except for the one that's stuck in my mind.

Waves roll in with giggling glee,
Each splash a challenge, come and see.
The sunburned skin is quite the sight,
While building sculptures takes all night.

Towels fly and sunscreen's thick,
All of our plans just seem to stick.
With ice cream cones that drip like rain,
And sticky fingers, fun's our gain.

When shadows stretch, we'll tell tall tales,
Of daring feats and crazy sails.
In our lost beach, we'd rather roam,
For laughter's the treasure that feels like home.

Tides of Tranquility

The shoreline sings a silly tune,
Where jellyfish dance to the moon.
We'll build a throne from driftwood logs,
And wave to passing froggy dogs.

Kites fly high with tales untold,
As we trade our worries for dreams of gold.
Each seagull's caw, a comical cheer,
Inviting laughter to draw near.

With snacks of chips and goofy drinks,
We ponder life while the ocean winks.
The tide pulls back, our feet embrace,
The sandy mess, a friendly trace.

As stars peek out, we gather 'round,
With stories shared and joy profound.
On the beach, we create our plight,
Where waves of giggles greet the night.

A Breezy Tale of Serenity

On a beach where seagulls scream,
I found my lost ice cream.
A flip-flop flew, oh what a sight,
As the tides laughed in pure delight.

With sunscreen smeared on my nose,
I danced like no one knows.
But the waves instead called my blunder,
As I tripped, fell, and rolled in thunder.

My hat flew off into the sea,
And a crab pinched my knee!
The sun upon my goofy grin,
As my adventure would begin.

Oh, the memories that we weave,
With laughter, joy, and a breeze.
For who knew fun could grow so free,
On a beach meant just for me?

Footprints in the Glittering Sand

I left my mark upon the shore,
Next to those who dance and snore.
With funky patterns, oh what fun,
Who knew footprints could be a pun?

With jellyfish doing the cha-cha,
I joined in, feeling like a star.
Laughing at a crab in a hat,
Spinning circles, now how about that?

Seashells whisper silly jokes,
While seagulls tease with funny pokes.
The surf keeps rhythm, a jazzy beat,
As waves crash down, a comical feat!

Amidst the sandcastles so grand,
I searched for treasure in the sand.
A bottle with a note inside,
"We're out of snacks! Come join the ride!"

Trails of a Relaxed Heart

With my toes in the water, I sit and muse,
Wishing my worries could just snooze.
A beach ball bounced right on my head,
The laughter echoed, no tears to shed.

A sunscreen battle, what a cruel fate,
Friends slathered me, a sticky mate.
But giggles erupted when I took a dive,
A fish gave me a look, like, 'How'd you survive?'

Drinks in hand, we toasted the sun,
Everyone stumbled, but it was all in fun.
Who needs a plan? Let's just wave,
For laughter's the treasure we all crave!

With toes twinkling in the soft-lit sand,
A hammock swayed as we made our stand.
Who knew relaxation could come with a cheer?
We'll reminisce over coconut beer!

Serenity's Sweet Dance

Under the sun with a frisbee thrown,
I blended moves with styles unknown.
A twist, a spin, oh what a sight,
As my dance partner took flight!

With starfish cheering from their post,
I tried to juggle a drink and toast.
Who knew that laughter could be so loud,
With my mischief-making friend so proud?

We sang to the seashells in our weird ways,
And even the tide joined in our plays.
As the sun dipped low and the sky turned pink,
We laughed till we cried, not stopping to think.

With each sunset, our spirits lifted high,
As seagulls danced in the evening sky.
In silly moments, joy's embrace,
We found our rhythm, our own sweet space!

Reverent Rhapsody of the Gulf

Seagulls gossiping, quite a sight,
Stealing fries with all their might.
A crab scuttles, fashionably late,
Wearing shells, it feels just great.

Fish dance in their shimmering schools,
Jellyfish float like playful fools.
A dolphin flips, with style it shows,
While sandcastles take on crazy foes.

Kids chase waves, a slippery spree,
Covered in sand, just like a bee.
Laughter echoes, pure delight,
As a bucket spills, what a sight!

Under the sun, we jump and shout,
Life's a beach, without a doubt.
From flip-flops flying to ice cream spills,
Every moment fills with silly thrills.

The Mosaic of Sunlit Desires

Sun hats bobbing, what a scene,
Dancing shadows, serene and keen.
Beach balls bounce like giant dreams,
While sunscreen's squirted in funny streams.

A sand dune's climb becomes a race,
Windblown hair, we laugh in grace.
Lemonade spills, sticky and bright,
Ants join in a silly bite.

Seashells whisper secrets of waves,
Surfboards wobble, it's like we're brave.
A sand angel flops, here and there,
With laughter hanging in the air.

Sunset paints the skies in pairs,
As we pose with silly glares.
A night of jest and goofy prance,
Memories made in joyous dance.

Kisses from the Coastal Winds

Winds that tickle, tease your hair,
Whispering secrets that float in air.
Kites soaring high, they wave goodbye,
As beachside ice creams melt with a sigh.

Sand splitters giggle, boats they chase,
While picnic baskets find their place.
Flip-flops flapping as they sprint,
Chasing umbrellas on a whimsical hint.

Seashells shining, treasures to find,
Crabs click-clack in a dance well-timed.
Kids dig deep, with cheerful shrills,
Transforming beaches to royal hills.

Laughter erupts, a joyous sound,
As we twirl in circles around and around.
In their embrace, we find pure bliss,
With every giggle, a salty kiss.

Tranquil Reflections at Dusk

As the sun dips, we start to sing,
Jokes about crabs take to wing.
Kites now rest, in colors so fine,
While snacks parade on the seaside line.

Footprints fading, memories bright,
The horizon blushes, a whimsical sight.
Beach towels folded, laughter confined,
Under the stars, hilarity unwind.

Shell collect, a mishap or two,
A fish that jumps, oh, how it flew!
Waves that giggle as they retreat,
Sharing tales of our sandy feat.

So we gather 'round, in soft twilight,
Belly laughs echo, pure delight.
In the calm, humor resounds,
And joy in the silence resounds.

Beyond Seashells and Stars

On the beach, I lost my shoe,
It ran off with a crab, who knew?
I chased it down, the sand did stick,
That pesky shellfish is quite a trick!

The seagulls squawk as they dive and swoop,
Stealing my fries, that silly troop!
I laugh and toss my sandwich high,
Next thing I know, it's caught in the sky!

My sunhat's blown, it takes to flight,
I shout, 'Come back!' with all my might.
It dances past, with such a flair,
Now it's the ocean's own millionaire!

Among the waves, a dolphin grins,
Wearing shades, and it spins to win.
"Catch me two points!" it says with glee,
As I slip and trip on a slippery sea!

The Warmth of Distant Horizons

In flip-flops bright, they squeak and sway,
Racing the tide, we shout, "Hooray!"
My friend's got sunburn, red as a shrimp,
He claims it's fashion, a goofy blimp!

A beach ball bounces, it's lost its air,
Rolling away, without a care.
We chase it down, through sand it flies,
Like a rebellious kid, oh what a prize!

The sunscreen battle, we laugh and squirt,
It looks like war paint on my shirt.
With each new splash, we giggle and dive,
The warmth of the sun makes us feel alive!

At sunset's glow, our shadows stretch,
Tracing the stories that life can fetch.
We dance like fools, free as the breeze,
Counting the grains, lost in the tease!

Parables from Saltwater Skies

Sandcastles rise, but then they fall,
A little wave gives them a brawl.
We laugh and rebuild, not a worry in sight,
Our kingdom of sand was quite the delight!

A hermit crab steals my buried lunch,
I yell, "Hey! That's not for your munch!"
It scuttles along, a sneaky little beast,
End of the picnic, time for a feast!

The lifeguard's whistle, a comic ruse,
Telling kids they can't swim in shoes.
But here we are, splashing away,
In our fancy footwear, come what may!

As kites soar high, we spin and twirl,
Each gust of wind makes our laughter whirl.
The ocean laughs back, a gurgle and glee,
Together we sing, a silly decree!

Symphony of the Retreating Waves

The waves roll in, then rush away,
A frothy dance, a silly ballet.
I slip and splash, a graceful fall,
The ocean giggles, it's quite the call!

With every tide, there's a joke to share,
The seaweed tickles, light as air.
I'll build a raft of beach debris,
Set sail for snacks, just wait and see!

A fish jumps high, wearing a cape,
It flops and flails, senior sea-drake!
We cheer it on, a finned superstar,
In our sandy seats, how glorious we are!

As night draws near, the stars peep down,
A twinkle, a wink, in the ocean's crown.
We join the moon, in this travelogue,
And snicker at crabs, in their silly dialogue!

Harbor of Eternal Bliss

In a boat made of dreams, we set sail,
With fish that gossip and crabs that wail.
The seagulls squawk jokes, a comical troupe,
While turtles dance like they're in a loop.

A parrot sells tickets for laughs and snacks,
While mermaids juggle sea shells with no cracks.
The waves giggle softly, tickling our toes,
As we sip on the sunshine, in whimsical prose.

Beneath the Coral Canopy

Under a roof of colorful fish,
We feast on the ocean's jello-like dish.
A turtle named Bob wears a sunhat too large,
While octopuses play cards, feeling the charge.

Crabs play the banjo, a sight to behold,
While sea urchins tell tales that never get old.
With laughter that bubbles, we swim with delight,
In this wacky realm where the sea feels just right.

Wings Over Serendipity

With wings made of laughter, we fly high and free,
With flamingos that skate on a salty sea spree.
A pelican's juggling, a real funny sight,
While dolphins tell punny tales, day turns to night.

Clouds wear sombreros, and rainbows play cards,
As breezes giggle softly, leaving us charred.
In this land where the silly meets blissful and bright,
We dance with the gulls, till we're lost in the light.

Colors of the Morning Tide

The sunrise spills colors, a painter's delight,
As crabs put on sunscreen, a comical sight.
The clams hold a concert, with shells for a stage,
While fish get their groove on, releasing their rage.

Starfish wear sunglasses, all cool and composed,
And seaweed does the cha-cha, quite unconposed.
We giggle and splash as the tide ebbs and flows,
In a world full of laughter, where happiness grows.

Enchantment Along the Reef's Edge

Crabs in tuxedos dance with glee,
A jellyfish sings karaoke,
Octopuses juggle, quite bizarre,
While seahorses ride a tiny car.

Parrots squawk jokes from coconut trees,
Where starfish play cards in the breeze,
A sea turtle drives a boat so slow,
While fish throw confetti to and fro.

The coral's a stage for the show's big night,
With dolphins as dancers, a truly grand sight,
Clownfish chuckle, "Aren't we so neat?"
With bubbles of laughter, the ocean's upbeat.

As the sun dips low and the laughter fades,
Crustaceans wrap up their escapades,
With a wink and a wave, they say goodbye,
For another day's fun beneath the sky.

Echoing Lullabies of the Tide

A whale hums tunes, a ballad so sweet,
While otters pursue their floating treat,
Seagulls drop shells with a clatter and clang,
Then laugh as they dance, oh the joy they sang!

Crabs hold a feast, but forget the bread,
So a sandcastle builder, he's left to dread,
The tide comes in with a mischievous grin,
Turning fine feasts to quick saucy swims.

Gulls gossip 'bout who swam the best race,
The starfish claim they've set the pace,
While turtles debate on fashion and flair,
Their shells all polished with utmost care.

At twilight they gather, a party of sorts,
To share silly tales from faraway ports,
A symphony grand of laughter and cheer,
Echoing sweetly for all who draw near.

Whispers of Celestial Waters

Moonlit waves play tricks on the eye,
Where fish wear hats and seagulls can fly,
A clam misplaces its very last pearl,
While dolphins debate on the best dance swirl.

A crab makes a joke that cracks up the shore,
With laughter echoing more and more,
Starfish whisper secrets under the waves,
While sea cucumbers find new cool caves.

Mermaids giggle, tangled in seaweed,
Preparing for parties with seashells to heed,
While barnacles serve the finest of snacks,
And turtles offer rides on their comfy backs.

As the tides change tales, laughter replays,
With each ebb and flow, like the sun's rays,
The sea holds a magic in bubbles and dreams,
Where jocund tides wash away mundane schemes.

Beneath the Golden Skies

Seashells chat, they gossip and giggle,
While fish play tag, dart and wiggle,
At sunset, the sea pops out a grin,
With colors of candy, where fun begins.

Crabs plan a parade of silly sorts,
With floats made of kelp, in oceanic courts,
Seagulls in sweatsuits, ready to race,
Cheer on their friends in a playful embrace.

Dolphins jump high, trying to impress,
As sea stars applaud, they're simply the best,
A conch shell sports its finest attire,
While waves spread joy, like a sweet choir.

In the twilight, they settle, tired yet bright,
With dreams of new antics to share by moonlight,
As laughter drifts on the cool evening breeze,
Beneath the gold skies, everyone's at ease.

The Allure of Forgotten Coastlines

In a land where seagulls squawk and cry,
Old sailors tell tales of fish that fly.
With crabs on stilts and starfish in hats,
The seaweed dances while the sea bass chats.

Beneath the waves, a mermaid's tease,
She lost her comb, now her hair's a breeze.
With jellyfish jokes that make you giggle,
And sea cucumbers ready to wiggle.

Sandcastles crumble in waves of glee,
Pails and shovels filled with fantasy.
A fish that sings, out of tune and loud,
Makes the crustaceans laugh, oh so proud!

So come and join this coastal spree,
Where laughter mixes with salty sea.
In every splash, a chuckle and cheer,
Forget your worries, let joy steer!

Tides that Whisper Journeys

On a beach where the shells play key,
Sand dollars gossip, sipping their tea.
With waves that giggle and roll in a rush,
Starfish do yoga—yes, it's quite the hush.

The tide likes to tickle the toes that walk,
While crabs do the cha-cha and dolphins talk.
Fish in tuxedos swim with delight,
Dancing in moonlight, oh, what a sight!

Seagulls squabble over crumbs from a snack,
While octopuses plan a little attack.
With ink in the air, they create a show,
As the mermaids chorus their underwater flow.

So gather your friends for a splashing good time,
Where the water is sweet, and flavors rhyme.
In this whimsical realm, let worries cease,
Join in the laughter, find your peace!

Ocean's Kiss and Sandy Embrace

The sand's a blanket, soft and warm,
As crabs compete in a race, no harm.
Seashells giggle, buried in deep,
Telling secrets of the ocean, while we peep.

Oh, waves that splash like tickling hands,
Carrying dreams from faraway lands.
While turtles wear sunglasses, looking quite cool,
The sunbeam surfer shows off his drool.

With dolphins jumping in a joyful spree,
Making waves as they glide, wild and free.
And pirate parrots squawking with flair,
Who needs treasure when laughter's the faire?

So let's make footprints, where dreams intertwine,
In a place where the sun and the sea align.
Embrace the humor, in nature's grand show,
With an ocean's kiss, let your worries go!

Rhapsody of the Twilight Shore

As dusk descends on the shimmering bay,
Crabs in a band start their evening play.
With glowworms twinkling, they light up the scene,
It's a concert of critters, who sing like a queen.

The tide brings reflections of jokes from the deep,
While flounders and flippers take turns in their leap.
A whale's got a vest, looking mighty fine,
With a bowtie of kelp, rocking sunset's design.

Seagulls in bowler hats gossip away,
While the fish throw a party, come join the ballet.
With barnacles baffled by laughter so grand,
In this weird world, it's all quite unplanned.

So wander these shores, let your spirit ignite,
In the rhapsody of twilight, life is just right.
With every wave, let your laughter soar,
In the joy of this moment, forever encore!

Cascades of Warm Seas

Waves that tickle toes in sand,
Seagulls squawking, feeling grand.
Flip-flops flying, what a sight,
As beach balls bounce with sheer delight.

Ice cream melting, it's a race,
Dancing crabs, they set the pace.
Sunburned noses, laughter flows,
In paradise, anything goes!

Sandcastles crumbling, oh what fun,
Shells are treasures for everyone.
Surfboards wobble, smiles abound,
With funny faces all around.

A beachside bar with fruity drinks,
Where everyone just laughs and winks.
With every splash and silly dive,
We know we're truly alive!

Mirage of the Tropic Sun

Palm trees waving, what a scene,
Bikinis blushing, if you know what I mean.
Sipping coconut, feeling fine,
While sunburnt tourists read the signs.

Flip-flops find the strangest places,
Some on feet, others in embraces.
Surfboards struggling in the tide,
With giggles echoing far and wide.

Tanning lotion, a slippery mess,
Rub it in, we all confess.
As sunscreen fights the beachy woes,
Squeaky laughs the whole day glows.

Oh, what joy beneath the rays,
In a land where merriment stays.
Keep the fun rolling, set the tune,
With every laugh, we chase the moon!

Treasures Beneath Wistful Waves

Bubbles rising, fish parade,
Toward the coral, we have strayed.
Flippers flapping, such a grace,
While dolphins giggle in the race.

Mermaids giggling, oh so sly,
Searching for pearls that can't say why.
With rubber ducks and snorkel dreams,
In twilight waters, nothing's as it seems.

Treasure maps that lead nowhere,
To mysterious spots filled with flair.
Sandy boots and goggles askew,
Synchronized swimming? Not for you!

We dive and splash in goofy cheer,
Finding seashells and seaweed beer.
With each silly tumble, we declare,
The ocean's magic is truly rare!

Beyond the Coastal Dunes

Kites a-soaring, with the breeze,
Sand between toes as we tease.
With laughter ringing near the shore,
Who needs a map when there's so much more?

Picnic baskets full of snacks,
With ants marching for their attacks.
Unexpected splashes from the waves,
As our laughter our spirits saves.

Surfing lessons, oh what a sight,
Falling down? An everlasting fight!
With every wipeout, cheers arise,
We know the sun will always rise.

Under the stars, the stories spin,
With goofy grins, the fun begins.
Gather your friends, the night is young,
With songs of joy forever sung!

The Harbor of Lost Souls

In a harbor where socks go to hide,
Forgotten by dryers and washed away tide.
The fish wear bow ties, quite fishy, I swear,
As sailors debate how to style their sea hair.

With seagulls who squawk in a befuddled tone,
They steal chips from your plate; it's their favorite throne.

Rats in top hats dance the cha-cha on docks,
While crabs play the banjo, a sight that unlocks.

The lighthouse beams jokes, brightening the night,
As rubber ducks race, giving seagulls a fright.
The mermaids throw parties, their laugh echoes loud,
While octopi juggle for the floating crowd.

So if you feel lost, just follow your nose,
To this quirky escape where the salty breeze blows.
With smiles all around, we can throw all our woes,
In a harbor of laughter, where anything goes!

Within the Embrace of the Tide

As waves roll and tumble in playful delight,
Sandy toes giggle beneath the moonlight.
Seashells speak secrets in languages strange,
While dolphins do flips with an elegant change.

The tide brings a treasure of mismatched old shoes,
That pair up with seaweed, it's quite the news!
Crabs practice ballet on shifting sand bars,
Winking at tourists from old rusty cars.

The breeze whispers stories of fish in disguise,
In sunglasses and hats, they gossip and rise.
With laughter like bubbles that pop in midair,
Each splash pulls us closer, we're caught unaware.

So come take a dip in this blue, silly land,
Where the giggles unroll like the soft, golden sand.
Embraced by the tide, let your troubles subside,
In this whirl of fun, let's merrily ride!

Emblem of Forgotten Journeys

Beneath a sky painted with cotton candy fluff,
Sailboats drift lazily, their journeys look rough.
But worry not, as we sip on some tea,
While mermaids poke fun at our knees that are free.

Maps lead us nowhere, they twist and they twirl,
Pointing to spots where we stumbled and swirled.
With rubber rafts bouncing as laughter we whirl,
The compass spins wildly, it's an amusing swirl.

Old pirates tell tales with a wink and a grin,
Of treasure that sparkles with every old spin.
But really, it's jellybeans they talk about,
As they dance with the seagulls, there's no room for doubt.

So grab your old suitcase, let's wander with glee,
Where even our flops bring us closer, you see.
An emblem of journeys, both silly and bright,
In this wondrous adventure, we'll shine in the light!

A Lullaby for the Weary Traveler

Close your eyes, dear friend, on the shores of a dream,
As waves hum a tune, like a soft, gentle stream.
Sandcastles nod off, in their cozy retreat,
While crabs tap their toes to the rhythm so sweet.

The stars wear pajamas; they blink with delight,
Guiding our thoughts through the velvety night.
A raccoon in pajamas is cradled by waves,
While jellyfish giggle, in luminescent caves.

Seagulls play checkers, with shells for the pieces,
In a game of great skill, but nobody fleeces.
As starfish recite silly poems in rhyme,
Making waves roll softly, as if telling time.

So drift on this lullaby, soft as a sigh,
Embrace all the wonders, let troubles float by.
For here in this moment, where laughter's the key,
The weary find joy, like shells by the sea!

Serenades of the Beachfront

With sand between our toes so bright,
We dance like crabs in morning light.
A seagull swoops, steals my snack,
And now my lunch plan's gone off track.

The waves are joking, 'Catch us if you can!'
While sunscreen's flying from my hand.
I slip and slide, oh what a sight,
Beach ballets gone wrong, pure delight!

A clam approaches, insisting on fun,
Claiming he's George, the beach's number one.
We laugh and cheer, we're all part of this team,
Giggling loudly, life's one funny dream.

As twilight falls, the bonfire glows,
With marshmallows charred, we strike silly poses.
Echoing laughter, the stars give a wink,
In this goofy paradise, we all love to think.

A Journey to Sublime Shores

I packed my bags with snacks galore,
Forgot the towel, now there's sand galore.
The boat's a-rocking, oh what a scene,
As fish swim by, laughing 'What do you mean?'

A pirate hat is blowing away,
Chasing it down, I trip, hooray!
The dolphins giggle, show off their flair,
While I'm swabbing decks and pulling my hair.

Seashells whisper secrets from the sea,
One claims it's a treasure, just wait and see.
But when I open it, what do I find?
A rubber chicken, of the silliest kind!

As sunset paints the world in gold,
We recount our antics, each story bold.
With laughter echoing through the night,
Our journey's a mess, but oh, what a sight!

Touch of the Horizon

The horizon drips in colors bright,
As seagulls argue, 'I'm taking that flight!'
We build a castle, but wind's not a friend,
Brick by brick, it soon meets its end.

A crab in armor declares it's the king,
Chasing the waves, it begins to sing.
We join in chorus, our voices a mess,
The beach becomes our grand stage, no less!

I spy a treasure, or so I think,
But it's just a flip-flop, that barely can sink.
What a toss of fate, my day has turned bright,
In this comical quest, let's dance through the night.

The stars are giggling as we all lay back,
Making up stories, filling the crack.
With each wave's laugh, the fun goes on,
In this silly paradise, we all belong!

Beneath a Canopy of Stars

Beneath the stars, we set up camp,
With s'mores in hand, feeling quite damp.
The fire's crackling, it thinks it's clever,
Playing on shadows like it's a river.

I attempt to fish with a stick and some rope,
But all I land is a slippery soap.
The tug of the water, the joy of the chase,
As fish gather round just to show off their grace.

A crab shares gossip, it's the latest trend,
While my marshmallow meets chocolate, my friend.
The sweet gooeyness, oh what a treat,
And laughter erupts with each little greet.

With blankets piled, and giggles galore,
We dream of adventures, what's next in store?
Under the canopy, the whole world seems light,
In our silly embrace, we dance through the night.

Reflections in the Gentle Surf

A crab pinches my toe, oh what a sight,
I dance like a fool, oh the sheer delight.
Sea gulls laugh, they caw with glee,
As I trip on the sand, who's watching me?

Flipping my flop, it flies in the breeze,
A shell lands on my head, oh, what a tease!
The water tickles, pulls at my feet,
The fish join the fun with a splash and a greet.

My drink takes a dive, it's now part of the tide,
A wave takes my hat, oh, how can I hide?
With laughter and splashes, the day is a blur,
Life's better with friends and a little bit of slur.

As sunset arrives, the sky starts to play,
Colors like confetti all shades of the day.
I'll recall this moment, forever long,
With a laugh, a splash, and a silly song.

An Odyssey of Starlit Waves

The beach is a circus, oh what a scene,
With sandcastles crumbling, looking quite mean.
A surfboard slips, and I take a big fall,
The waves giggle softly, oh, do they have gall?

A starfish waves back, trying to blend,
I ask for directions, it just can't comprehend.
Fish in a school, they gossip away,
As I ponder my life and the things they might say.

My sunscreen's a mess, I look like a ghost,
I sneak past the seagulls, they're plotting the roast.
A jellyfish glows, it boogies in the surf,
It's a groovy little party, oh, full of mirth.

Under starlit skies, where the wild waves play,
I make new friends, in the sand we may stay.
A laugh at this life, floating on beams,
In tides of humor, we drift in our dreams.

The Enchanted Lagoon

A frog in a hat, oh what a surprise,
Compliments my sandals, and claims it's no lies.
The palm trees party, they sway to the beats,
While dolphins do flips, they're stealing the seats.

Mermaids peek shyly, with glittery hair,
Playing peek-a-boo from their watery lair.
I wave a hello, but they shriek with delight,
My float's an ice cream, and it's melting just right.

The sun's a big ball of friendly old fun,
As crabs do the cha-cha, oh don't they run?
My picnic's a mess, with ants on the spree,
Each crumb's a banquet for guests, oh my glee!

Under tropical skies, the laughter persists,
With jellybeans tossed, we hop and we twist.
In this magical retreat, life takes a fling,
With laughter and joy, let's dance and just sing.

Dance of the Tidal Spirits

The tides have a rhythm, a jig in the blue,
They tease and they swirl, oh, how they do!
With a hop and a splash, the beach balls fly,
I join the dumb dance while the seagulls just sigh.

A sea cucumber wants to take lead of the show,
But trips on a seashell and goes down below.
A starfish is laughing, with such tiny hands,
While I'm cracking up, rolling in the sands.

The wind plays the piano, soft notes in the air,
As jellyfish waltz, filled with musical flair.
They twirl under moonlight, all shimmer and shine,
I wonder if this silly night could be mine.

From dawn until dusk, we whirl with the tides,
With chuckles and grace, where fun never hides.
In this whimsical dance, joy's wild and free,
Our hearts are the beats, let's sway by the sea.

Fragments of a Halcyon Dawn

Woke up early, not a creature in sight,
Seagulls are cackling, what a silly fright!
Coffee's too strong, it's dancing in my cup,
Stirring up dreams, oh, let's fill them up!

Sunshine bursts in, all golden and bright,
Flip-flops are squeaking, oh what a delight!
Tripping on sand, I do the cha-cha slide,
A crab joins in—my unexpected guide!

Waves are giggling, splashing with fun,
Making me blush like a ripe summer bun.
The tide pulls back, then gives me a wink,
Oh no, my sandwich! Come back, I can't think!

But here in the morning, with laughter abound,
Life's a wild circus with funny sounds.
Fragments of joy in the radiant heat,
Dancing and spinning—oh, isn't life sweet?

The Call of Glimmering Waters

A shrimp in a tux jumps right on my plate,
His dance is so charming, can't make him wait!
I lean in closer, he offers a grin,
But all of his friends are just waving... come in!

Mermaids are laughing, though I see no tails,
Just a guy in a speedo, regaling tall tales.
The fish roll their eyes as he shimmies away,
Glimmers of laughter, in bubbles they play.

The crab in the corner just rolled up his sleeves,
He's taken up yoga—yes, that's what he believes!
Stretching his claws, he reaches for a snack,
Don't mind me too much, I just might attack!

Oh, the ocean's a stage, and everyone's here,
Each wave tells a joke while the sun takes a beer.
I sip at my drink as the tides ebb and flow,
Finding hilarity where we least expect it to show.

Reveries of the Coastal Breeze

Kites are a-flying, but mine seems to land,
Perched on a seagull—ah, that wasn't planned!
Chasing it down, I get tangled in lines,
A tangle of laughter, oh! Who needs designs?

Shells whisper secrets from deep in the sand,
While I slip and slide—didn't think I was planned!
Saltwater sprinkles me, oh, what a prank,
I'll be fresh as a daisy, or so I think, pranked!

The breeze tells me stories of old sailors lost,
But I just want snacks, no matter the cost.
A burger gone rogue rolls away with a laugh,
Chasing my lunch—a new form of a gaffe!

Under a sun hat that's two sizes too big,
I dance with the wind like a comical fig.
Reveries shimmer like dreams in the breeze,
Wrapped in the laughter of the ocean's tease.

Gifts from the Glistening Horizon

Oh look at that pelican, such a fine sight,
He steals my sandwich—I'm not the least bit uptight!
It's funny how feathers can make a swift snack,
I'll just swap for a donut—hey, that's my knack!

Surfboards are crashing, the riders all giggle,
Falling like jelly, it's hard not to wiggle.
Each tumble a treasure, each splash a delight,
Catching the laughter in waves of sheer light.

A conch shell of wisdom rolls up to my toes,
With gossip from dolphins, who really just pose.
They flash me a grin, and I'm feeling the cheer,
What gifts from afar, bring the sunshine so near!

The sun starts to dip, all golden and round,
The laughter still echoes, it knows no bound.
Gifts from a horizon where fun takes its flight,
Joy wrapped in laughter—what a splendid night!

Visions Carved by Tidal Hands

Waves crash down with playful glee,
Creating castles for all to see.
But just one sneeze, and poof! They're gone,
A sandy throne for the gull upon.

Seashells sing in a silly tune,
While crabs dance under a cheeky moon.
Starfish giggle as they wiggle about,
Who knew the ocean's party was so loud?

The seaweed sways like hairy locks,
While jellyfish float in silly socks.
The tides conspire, what a funny sight,
With sea anemones ready for a fight!

So next time you tread where waters play,
Remember the jesters in their ballet.
Embrace the laughter in salty air,
And join the fun, if you dare!

Kaleidoscope of Oceanic Hues

Blue crabs wearing tiny hats,
Skitter sideways, like acrobatic brats.
Seahorses prance in a rainbow dance,
Twisting and swirling, what a silly chance.

The corals giggle in vibrant glitch,
Underwater's theme is decidedly kitsch.
Clown fish poke their heads with a grin,
As octopus juggle with matters of fin.

They laugh and splash, oh what a sight,
In this salty realm, all wrong feels right.
The waves join in with a cheerful cheer,
In a colorful world, there's nothing to fear!

So dive on down, let your worries float,
Join the party on this zany boat.
With hues and giggles that never cease,
In this grand oceanic piece of peace.

Beneath the Moonlit Veil

The moon hangs low, a big old pie,
Reflecting laughter as fish swim by.
Crickets serenade in rhythmic beats,
While turtles bust moves in funky feats.

Mermaids whisper silly secrets near,
Trading seashells and giggles with cheer.
With a wink and a splash, they flip and twirl,
Oh, the underwater antics unfurl!

The night tides swirl like a swanky ball,
With seaweed laced gowns for one and all.
Starry-eyed dolphins leap with grace,
Shining bright in this cheeky place.

So if you find a patch of soft sand,
Join the night's fun, don't you just stand!
The whimsy awaits, so take a dive,
Beneath the giggles where spirits thrive.

Celestial Driftwood and Endless Light

Driftwood dances, a celebrity star,
Floating past jellyfish playing guitar.
The sun sets low, casting golden rays,
On this ridiculous stage where sea life plays.

Sandcastles wear crowns, they puff up with pride,
As the tide rolls in, they laugh and slide.
Seagulls parade with pizzazz in flight,
Chasing each other in mock feathered fights.

The breeze carries tales from the ocean's core,
Of mermaid mischief and legendary lore.
So let your heart laugh with the bubbles that rise,
In this tranquil realm where joy never dies.

As the stars twinkle like winking eyes,
Join the fun in this ocean surprise.
With driftwood and dreams shining so bright,
Embrace the silliness, bask in the light!

Tidal Dreams and Sunlit Shores

Seagulls laugh, the beach is bright,
A crab in shades, what a sight!
Beach balls bounce, oh what a race,
Sandy toes in a goofy chase.

Waves that splash with joy abound,
A wave rider's lost, yet found!
Sunburned noses, sunscreen mess,
Each day surprises, we confess.

Barefoot dances, in the sun,
Oops, fell down—now that's just fun!
Laughter echoes, kids at play,
Every moment makes our day.

Flip-flops fly, they take a trip,
Watch them soar—a wobbly flip!
Under umbrellas, we just lay,
Napping dreams by the bright bay.

Flavors of the Azure Bay

Ice cream drips on sandy feet,
Chocolate sprinkles taste so sweet!
A seagull steals a soda pop,
Chasing it makes my heart stop.

Fish that dance in the cool tide,
With little hats, they swim with pride!
Coconut laughs, a fruity cheer,
Waves cheer on, they love to hear.

Sandcastles made, but oh, they fall,
The tide just smirks, it claims them all!
Silly seashells with winking eyes,
Whisper secrets to the skies.

Picnic spreads with giggles loud,
Who knew we'd feast amongst this crowd?
Lemonade spills, what a delight,
As evening glows, we feel just right.

Woven Lore of Serene Waters

The ocean whispers tales untold,
Of mermaids dressed in gold a bold!
Clams recite their ancient rhymes,
Crabs do the jig with one thin time.

A dolphin dives in search of fun,
Flipping high, he's number one!
On the beach, we chase a kite,
In the breeze, our worries take flight.

Starfish laugh in the ebbing surf,
Tickling toes gives us much smurf!
Treasure maps drawn in the sand,
Lead to silly finds—oh so grand.

Under the moon, our shadows sway,
Sharing stories in a silly way.
Each wave tells us to stay awhile,
In laughter's grip, we share a smile.

Oceanic Tales of Peace

Bubbles rising, fish on the run,
Chasing tales in the midday sun!
A pirate hat on a sunburned head,
In this treasure zone, we forge ahead.

Sandy snacks and giggly glee,
Who knew snack time could be so free?
Shells collected, each one a prize,
With goofy grins, we improvise.

A hammock swings, caught in a breeze,
As sunbeams dance among the trees.
Tales of squids in polka dots,
Make us chuckle, forget our thoughts.

At twilight's glow, a crab parade,
Sideways strut in a joyful cascade!
Here we gather, hearts full of cheer,
In this haven, life feels clear.

Where Dreams Meet the Sea

A jellyfish danced with a wobbly stare,
While crabs in tuxedos sipped salty air.
The fish wore sunglasses, a sight to behold,
And whispered wild tales of treasures untold.

Seagulls with hats squawked the latest news,
As octopuses grooved in their polka dot shoes.
The tide tickled toes, a playful embrace,
While shells organized a rhythmic race.

Mermaids served tacos with laughter and cheer,
And dolphins brought cocktails, oh what a smear!
But watch out for seaweed, it's tricky to shake,
Those slippery greens can cause quite the lake!

Under a moon that winks with delight,
The sandcastles bow down, it's quite the sight.
So come with your friends, let's frolic and play,
Where dreams swirl like waves, come dance away.

Luminous Tide and Starlit Skies

The wave crested high, like a giant balloon,
While crabs set the stage for a beachside tune.
Starfish in glitter, they grooved all around,
Their dance moves were silly, but joy was profound.

A clam tried to rap, but it was quite slow,
With seaweed as backup, they stole the show.
Fish formed a chorus, all singing in glee,
While a walrus rolled by, squawking, "Look at me!"

Under the glow of the shimmering light,
The starry-eyed turtles had a dance-off that night.
Shells clapped with laughter, the ocean was bright,
As critters united in joyous delight.

With laughter like bubbles that floated on by,
Seagulls performed acrobatics up high.
So grab your beach towel, let's join in the sound,
Where luminous waters and giggles abound.

Embracing the Serene Abyss

In the depths of the sea where the clams like to sing,
A turtle in shades claimed the crown, the king.
He ruled over fish who wore bowties with flair,
While starfish applauded in their polka dot wear.

An octopus chef stirred a soup with great zeal,
That made all the mermaids do a happy wheel.
They flipped and they flopped in the glow of the moon,
While eels played the drums, setting quite the tune.

But lurking nearby was a shark with a plan,
To crash the big party, he thinks he's the man.
Yet, with a swift wiggle, a flounder said, "No!"
And soon they were all doing the limbo below.

So join in the fun where the waters run deep,
With laughter and fish stories you'll never keep.
In a world so peculiar, where mischief's the muse,
We find joy in the depths, let's cut loose and cruise!

Secrets Beneath Sapphire Skies

Under sapphire waves where the secrets lay hidden,
A sea turtle giggled, "What have I been bidden?"
With each gentle ripple, new tales start to form,
As dolphins play peek-a-boo in perfect swarm.

A pirate fish pondered on treasures unseen,
While seahorses laughed, sipping seaweed cuisine.
They played a grand game of hide and seek fun,
Then celebrated victories with aquatic pun.

Crab told tall tales of the beach and its charm,
With a wink and a nudge, he sang with great alarm.
The sun painted smiles on each fishy face,
While jellyfish jived, floating through endless space.

So come to the ocean, where laughter's the key,
Where bubbles of joy are setting us free.
With secrets and smiles, let's dance every tide,
Under sapphire skies, come enjoy this ride!

www.ingramcontent.com/pod-product-compliance
Lightning Source LLC
Chambersburg PA
CBHW072214070526
44585CB00015B/1333